13 March 1944, Russian soldiers, ankle deep in mud, inspect a Panther Ausf.A left behind by the Germans in Uman, Ukraine. This is the same Panther featured in *Panzerwrecks 5*, at the top of page 54, and has the rare tow coupling introduced in November 1943. The distinctive horizontal 'Zimmerit' indicates it is a rarely photographed Demag vehicle. Uman was a popular site for Russian propagandists, and a harbinger of the German retreats to follow in the summer of 1944. **RGAKFD**

A hobbled Pz.Kpfw.IV Ausf.H, circa 1943 production, made it only so far in the recovery process before being abandoned. It has the cylindrical 'Filzbalgvorschaltluftfilter' plus 'Zimmerit' but lacks the side vision ports in the superstructure. Oddly enough, the lid on the commander's cupola opens almost horizontally (compare to others in this book). Markings consisted of a simple cross and tactical number '533'. The two vehicles here have been 'short-tracked' for two reasons: first so that the drive train, wheels and other parts didn't receive any further damage, and secondly because often without the tracks there was too much rolling resistance for the 'Zugkraftwagen' to overcome. **RGAKFD**

Russian motorised troops carry on the pursuit while others pick through the worn out Panzers and assault guns. We can see here (lower left) that the Pz.Kpfw.IV from the previous page has been short-tracked on one side only, and that all the vehicles carry a dirty coat of winter whitewash. **3x RGAKFD**

A lesson in 'tactics and terrain' is being taught to an attentive student using visual aids such as this Pz.Kpfw.IV with its ghostly tactical number.

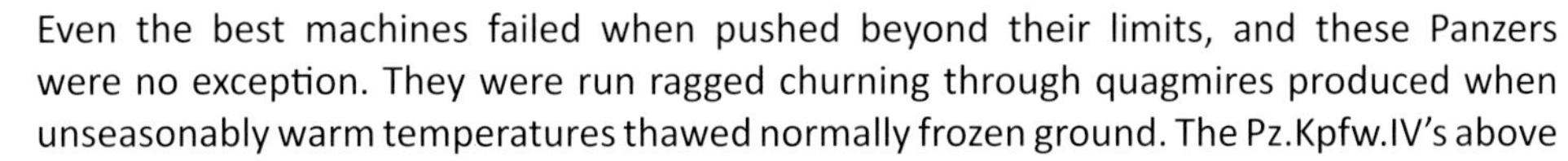

Even the best machines failed when pushed beyond their limits, and these Panzers were no exception. They were run ragged churning through quagmires produced when unseasonably warm temperatures thawed normally frozen ground. The Pz.Kpfw.IV's above soldiered on but succumbed like the others to drive train failure and other mechanical breakdowns. The Panthers below have experienced significant damage to their hulls as well. **3x RGAKFD**

Panthers of SS-Pz.Rgt.3, 3.SS.Panzer-Division lie knocked out south of Ostburg (Polish name Pułtusk), Poland in October 1944. According to the photograph's caption they were knocked out by Soviet artillery, although it is quite possible that this was a collection or repair centre as all of the tanks have some sort of running gear related problem. The close up of tank '435' on page 7 shows the 'Totenkopf' divisional insignia of the 3.SS next to the radio operator's MG, a very unusual sight on a Panther. 'SS' runes and a date are painted in white on the front fender. Note the three AP scoops in the lower nose armour. The 'tile' pattern of 'Zimmerit' indicates a Daimler-Benz manufactured vehicle. **3x RGAKFD**

435

A Pz.Sfl.1 für 7.62cm Pak36 sits on a railway wagon in Odessa, Ukraine, March 1944. The scruffy coat of whitewash has worn off of the gun barrel and was not applied at all on the Balkenkreuz on the hull side. Spare track has been fixed across the front of the 14.5mm thick armour of the fighting compartment. The only unit equipped with these vehicles in the H.Gr.A sector was Pz.Jg.Abt.721.

RGAKFD

An excellent example of a Panzerjäger II für 7.5cm Pak 40/2 (Sd.Kfz.131), photographed in Hungary in 1945. The oakleaf insignia on the front of the fighting compartment indicates that this belonged to Pz.Jg.Abt.37 of 1.Panzer-Division. What looks like the number '9' is more likely to be a '2' as it has a tail, and is probably German. The number '115' on the gunshield is a Russian trophy identification number. Note the large boxes on the engine compartment and the wire threaded around the vehicle to tie down camouflage materials.

A 'Wespe' and 'Hummel' lie wrecked in Brandenburg, 1945, their destruction courtesy of forces of the 1st Byelorussian Front. The 'Hummel' has the extended driver's compartment introduced in early 1944 and steel return rollers. It would appear to have run over a mine as it is missing the front roadwheels and has a broken track. **RGAKFD**

A Munitionspanzer 'Wespe' shoved into a ditch in Hungary, 1945. While being pushed into its resting place, the vehicle's roadwheels have come out from between the guide-horns of the tracks. Two of these vehicles were issued to every 'Wespe' battery and could be converted to a normal 'Geschützwagen II' if required.

More wreckage in Hungary, this time a Pz.Kpfw.III Ausf.L with much of its running gear missing and the hull of a Pz.Kpfw.IV behind. The Pz.Kpfw.III has the faint outline of the tactical number '611' on the turret side, the tops of the '1's being particularly long.

An unusual sight, especially at this point in the War. A gr.Pz.Bef.Wg.Ausf.K (Sd.Kfz.267 or 268) photographed near Lake Balaton in 1945. The only reported loss of a Pz.Bef.Wg.III in the period 15 January to 15 March 1945 was from 1.Panzer-Division. The small hatch on the turret roof for the 'Kurbelmast' is open and the vision port on the turret side is missing. The two vehicles in the background are a Jagdpanzer 38 and a Sturmgeschütz III.

Northwest of Nagy-Perkáta, Hungary, is a Bergepanther that, according to the caption, was destroyed by a 76mm shell. In spite of being a very poor quality photograph we can see the 'V' shaped brackets left behind when the wood plank bridge atop the superstructure burned away. The vehicle lacks the rear spade, but has the mounts for it at the bottom of the rear plate. It is unusual for a recovery vehicle to have a tactical number; this one appears to have '502' painted on the side. **TsAMO**

The wreck of what we believe is a Munitionspanzer IV. The front of the vehicle has copious amounts of spare track: note how the track sits flat over the ball mounted MG - perhaps this was removed? Armament appears to be an MG on a pintle which can be seen above the driver's position. The fenders may have been reinforced by braces from the superstructure as one is visible on the far side of the vehicle. A 'fence' has been erected around the sides and rear of the engine deck and some fuel cans can be seen there. The 1.Panzer-Division lost 3 'Mun-Träger IV' during March 1945. Perhaps we have one here?

Pz.Art.Rgt.13, 13.Panzer-Division lost this 'Hummel' in Hungary. The armour around the fighting compartment has been blown off and part of it is lying next to the wreck. This section of armour carries the divisional insignia on a black background (see inset photo). The rear hull has snapped off but is still attached to the vehicle by the track. One leg of the rear gun travel lock is still attached to both gun and hull side.

2x TsAMO

A 'Hummel', or what is left of it after a catastrophic explosion. The left side of the fighting compartment with the letter 'C' painted onto it is in the foreground. The two circular objects by the gun mount are the remains of the equilibrators. Photographed in Hungary in 1945.

Peasants from nearby villages view destroyed German armour at the railway station in Chernivtsi, Ukraine, at the end of March, 1944. Chernivtsi is 40km east of the Carpathian Mountains and about 60km east of the Hungarian border, and in March of 1944 3rd Guards Tank Army of the 1st Ukranian Front drove due south from Dubno to Chernivtsi between the Seret and Zbruch Rivers, cutting several major rail lines along the way. These rail lines were the Germans' main method of evacuation and reinforcement, and, once cut, troops on the wrong side, such as those manning these Pz.Kpfw.IV's and StuG III's, were systematically encircled and eliminated. Here a badly damaged Sturmgeschütz Ausf.G, with its broken drive sprocket and missing roof, seems to have been shot up in place. Behind it is an Ausf.F/8 backfitted with 'Schürzen'. **3x RGAKFD**

A new Pz.Kpfw.IV Ausf.J with its turret at 6 o'clock. It looks like the driver's hatch has been propped up in front of his visor. Because these vehicles have no identifying numbers or insignia we cannot tell which unit they belonged to except to say they were in First Panzer Army's sector when the end came. **RGAKFD**

The opposite view of the previous page shows the second Pz.Kpfw.IV in more detail. Here we see all the hatches open for inspection, right down to the small hatch in the rear engine armour that allowed the fan drive to be disengaged during cold starts. This vehicle has the cast idler and steel return rollers. **RGAKFD**

The Pz.Kpfw.IV Ausf.J's appear to have arrived just in time to be knocked out, as the decision to drop the auxiliary generator set for the electrical turret traverse was made in February of 1944 and here we are a month later. The hole for the auxiliary generator's muffler is plugged by a large conical plug and a new coat of 'Zimmerit' applied. Interestingly enough, several rounds have punched through the turret skirt armour leaving perfect holes but no deformations in the thin steel. **RGAKFD**

Smoke candles have been set off to heighten the effect for the photographer as he captures these Pz.Kpfw.IV's on film. The smoke obscures the extensive damage to the left side of the vehicle: note the cracks in the bow armour, the separation of the front and side superstructure plates and the twisted railing for the 'Schürzen'. **2x RGAKFD**

This Pz.Kpfw.IV also has a hatch propped up in front of the driver's visor. Damage this time is on the right side where the skirt armour has been shot away and the rubber on the roadwheels reduced to ash by fire. Note how the tow cables run from the front tow shackles along the sides of the vehicle. **RGAKFD**

Soldiers of the 3rd Ukrainian Front check out a 7.5cm round from this Sturmgeschütz III Ausf.G, photographed on the road to Nikopol, Ukraine in 1944. The vehicle has been readied for Winter operations with the addition of a coat of whitewash over the paintwork and 'Mittelstollen' (ice sprags) on the one remaining track. Nikopol was liberated in early February 1944.

RGAKFD

The photos on this and the opposite page are of the same Panther Ausf.G, tactical number '201'. Note the mount on the commander's cupola for an AA MG and a crew member's seat on the turret roof. The photo opposite shows damage to the running gear and a shiny idler wheel from contact with the tracks. Based on the location of the 'Balkenkreuz', this Panther is one of the last M.N.H .manufactured vehicles produced prior to the cancellation of 'Zimmerit' application in the first half of September 1944. It appears a small pennant has been fitted into the 'pilze' on the right front corner of the turret roof.

1x EFA, 1x LVKFFDA 16508N

Main photo: A Panther Ausf.G is checked out by curious Russian soldiers and tank crews (note their padded tankers helmets). A horseshoe has been fitted on the rainguard over the gunner's periscope, although it brought them little in the way of luck. **Inset**: An older Ausf.A, possibly at the same unknown location as it is from the same collection.

2x L.Archer

A Panther Ausf.G captured intact by soldiers of the 3rd Byelorussian Front in East Prussia, 1945. The most notable feature of this tank is the combination of standard exhaust pipe and a 'Flammenvernichter' muffler! Other than that it is a fairly straightforward Panther with a chin mantlet, a raised fan housing for the crew compartment heater and no 'Zimmerit'. The tank has been emptied of its ammunition which is lying on the engine deck.

RGAKFD

An interesting Sturmgeschütz III Ausf.G. This vehicle was one of 170 built on the chassis of a Pz.Kpfw.III Ausf.J or L during 1944, as corroborated by the hull escape hatch. A small calibre projectile has penetrated the side of the superstructure, removing the 'Zimmerit' coating and damaging the track guard and 'Schürzen' rail in the process. The vehicle has concrete for extra protection on the side of the commander's cupola and a coaxial MG hole in the gun mantlet. The sign on the signal box in the background reads Kroßwitz, now known as Krośniewice in Poland. StuG.Lehr-Brig.920 passed through there during their retreat to Germany. **RGAKFD**

Panthers in the snow. Soldiers of the 3rd Ukrainian Front walk among the wrecks of Panther Ausf.A's on 27 February 1944. The tank in the main image and the lower right are probably the same vehicle - note the icicles hanging from the gun barrel and track guards.
3x RGAKFD

A Pz.Kpfw.IV Ausf.J photographed by a Russian technical intelligence team lies knocked out in Budapest City Park in January 1945. The tank was probably assembled during October 1944 as it has a pivoting cupola hatch and 'Drahtgeflecht-Schürzen' (wire mesh skirts) - although only the mounts remain. Parts used for modifications made during the production run were on a last in first out basis which explains why this tank has four return rollers, tubular welded idler and regular exhaust muffler. **2x TsAMO**

Tiger '934' of 9./SS-Pz.Rgt.3 that according to its caption was knocked out between Bicske and Baracksa in Hungary by a hit to the left of the hull from a 76mm anti tank gun. The SS-Pz.Rgt.3 was certainly in this area (from 21 January 1945), but according to *Tigers in Combat 2* sustained no losses there. According to the same source, however, two Tigers were knocked out on 6 January between the villages of Mány and Zsámbék according to the same source. Perhaps the Russian intelligence team lost their bearings? The tank has a very war-torn look, with flattened track guards and a shredded turret bin.

TsAMO

The front of the Tiger shows a penetration on its nose, with an AP scoop underneath. It would take a hit from a 122mm projectile or larger to make a hole in the Tiger's 102mm thick armour. A light covering of snow picks up the details of the 'Zimmerit' coating. *Tigers in Combat 2* goes on to say that the two Tigers were subsequently used as a command post for the 3.Kavallerie-Brigade.

TsAMO

Two shots into the engine compartment have stopped this Sturmgeschütz IV, photographed on a road in East Prussia in January 1945. The explosion has blown off the exhaust pipes, fractured the rear plate and rearranged the 'Schürzen'. The 'Schürzen' are unusual in that they have been modified by the unit to pivot. Other examples can be found in *Panzerwrecks 3* and *5*. The condition of the tracks would seem to indicate that it had not seen prolonged combat. Note the three return rollers and four rather than six bolts across the top of the suspension units.

RGAKFD

Pages 37-39: A sorry looking Pz.Kpfw.IV Ausf.H from 10./Pz.Rgt.24 of 24.Panzer-Division in Hungary during the Winter of 1944. Two lucky shots from the guns of the 2nd Ukrainian Front have perforated the gun barrel rendering it useless. The tank has been partially stripped as a number of wheels have been removed and there is no sign of the tracks. One of the drive sprockets can be seen propped up against the turret access hatch on page 39.
3x RGAKFD

1024

Two Tiger II's of an unidentified unit sit on a Hungarian road on a sunny day in 1945. The tanks were geographically close to each other as they have consecutive trophy numbers from a Russian technical intelligence team. Both vehicles have been painted white on their extremities to make them more visible. Tank '193' has its final drive housing sitting on the engine deck and tank '194' is missing its final drive and the toothed ring from its drive sprocket. These photographs have been retouched at some point in their lives.

A Panther Ausf.G captured in Hungary in 1945. This is a Panther with a difference as it has a sheet metal box on the rear plate for stowing infra-red equipment. This box conforms to the shape of a standard stowage bin and here the details are reasonably clear. The tank has a faint tactical number of '433' and Russian trophy number '219' painted on the turret side. This vehicle appears in the background of page 45.

As this Panzer IV/70(A) has four return rollers we can deduce that it was probably manufactured pre December 1944 and knowing that it was photographed in the Lake Balaton area means that it either belonged to 8./Pz.Rgt.6 of 3.Panzer-Division or 4./ Pz.Rgt.23 (who received them from 9./Pz.Rgt.24 of 24.Panzer-Division). Like other vehicles in this book it has been 'short-tracked' around the remaining roadwheels, return rollers and idler by the 'I-Staffel' (maintenance units). A careful look at the opened hatches on the roof of the fighting compartment will show a 'Vorsatz-P' mount in the loader's hatch. In the background is a Tiger II which is shown in detail on the next page.

A Tiger II at the same weapons collection point in Hungary. The tactical number of '?23' is indicative of s.SS-Pz.Abt.501. The number '200' was applied by a Russian technical intelligence team. This Tiger looks to be in generally good order; just missing a few sections of track guard from the side. Next to it is a Pz.Kpfw.IV Ausf.J, identifiable by the lack of muffler on the left rear plate for the auxiliary electrical generator. Both gun barrels show signs of having been retouched on the photograph.

This is the other side of the Pz.Kpfw.IV showing its Russian 'trophy' number '201'. Other than a solitary 'Balkenkreuz' on the side of the turret 'Schürzen', the tank has no markings, so it is impossible to say who it belonged to. The crew have added a little extra insurance to the sides using spare track links. The length of the Tiger's gun barrel is quite obvious in this shot, as it overhangs that of the Pz.Kpfw.IV. Note the Panther Ausf.G in the background from page 42.

At the same location as the vehicles on the four previous pages is Panther '122', a text book example of a late production Ausf.G, with no 'Zimmerit' coating, raised fan heater on the engine deck and 'Flammvernichter' mufflers on the exhausts. The entire front curved portion of the track guard is missing. The diagonal factory applied camouflage scheme is a Daimler-Benz pattern.

A weary looking Panzer IV/70(V) in Hungary. It is missing a suspension unit and the 'Schürzen' on the side of the engine compartment. A Russian 'trophy' number of '223' has been painted on the gun mantlet and by manipulating the image we can see a faint though indiscernible tactical number on the side.

A Sturmgeschütz III Ausf.G has been pushed off of the road after having a track creep off of its drive sprocket - see the track on the left, in the ditch. Like many other Panzers in this book, it had been abandoned after the failure of Unternehmen 'Frühlingserwachen' (Spring Awakening) around Lake Balaton, Hungary, in March 1945. The tracks are the wide 'Ostketten' introduced in 1944. Most of the 'Schürzen' plates are missing except for the one on the side of the superstructure. The centre section seen here was made up of two 5mm plates, one in front of the other. From this angle the commander's cupola should be visible; perhaps the roof has been blown off?

More 'Ostketten', but only on the sides and nose of this Sturmgeschütz III Ausf.G. It has a thick application of concrete over the top of the driver's compartment and around the commander's cupola. In reality, the concrete added extra weight but little extra protection. Interestingly there are tracks over the driver's compartment as you can see the track horns poking through the concrete. The front section of the track guard is missing.

A Flakpanzer IV 'Möbelwagen' knocked out during 'Unternehmen Frühlingserwachen'. The 25mm side plate has been holed by something and is held up by a post. The mesh covered frame in the foreground is the spent case collector cage which should be fitted to the rear right side of the 3.7cm Flak 43. A German helmet with the Russian trophy number is hanging from something on the nearside fender. It is thought that this Flakpanzer belonged to s.H.Pz.Abt.509.

A rear view of another Flakpanzer IV 'Möbelwagen' presumably lost in the same operation. The 'Flammentöter' exhausts are unusual in that they are angled at the top. The vehicle is a dark colour, this may be as a result of a fire. The starter crank in position and opened engine deck cover tell a story of a Flakpanzer broken down, then sabotaged.

Plight of the bumble bee. Ironically this 'Hummel' was knocked out by Soviet artillery near Lvov in July of 1944. The explosion has blown away the superstructure and part of the rear hull, leaving the gun mount exposed. The Pz.Art.Rgt.80 of 8.Panzer-Division was the only 'Hummel' equipped unit fighting in this area and lost 8 of these vehicles during July.

2x RGAKFD

The photos on pages 54 - 60, dated 13 March 1945, represent some of the finest images of late war Hungarian armour available, and while none of them arrived with captions, readers should be able to pick out extremely fine details as to their construction, camouflage and markings. The vehicle foremost on this page is a 40.M Turán medium tank, (40.M Turán közepes harekocsi), or Turán I, armed with a 4cm MÁVAG M.41 main gun and two 8mm Gebauer MG 34/40 A.M. It shares many construction features of the Pz.Kpfw.35(t), from its suspension to its riveted construction, but was actually based on Škoda's T-21 prototype design with an 8-cylinder engine (which doubled the available hp) and toothed sprocket front and rear. This particular vehicle had tactical number '2311', registration number '1H 218' (on the front plate over the machine gun), and a large number '7' in white next to the driver's visor. A 4cm round appears over the driver's position. The driver's hatch on the Turán I opened side to side. Note the complete absence of direct vision ports in the turret hatch door and elsewhere on these vehicles.

RGAKFD

A head-on view of a 41.M Turán heavy tank, (41.M Turán néhez harekocsi), or Turán II, armed with a short 7.5cm MÁVAG 41.M cannon and two machine guns. The roof in front of the commander's cupola was sloped to allow room for the bigger gun breech, and the driver's hatch, hinged in the middle, opened front to back. This vehicle carried tactical number '3211', registration number '1H 083' and an inverted white triangle by the machine gun, and a large shield and the number '10' next to the driver's visor. Originally it was thought that registration numbers starting with '1H' referred to tanks in the 'medium' class and numbers starting with '2H' referred to tanks in the 'heavy' class, but here we see that disproved. The inverted triangle is believed to have represented 2.Páncéloshadostály (2nd Armoured Division). The markings on the right side are claimed to represent the 3rd Rgt. 10th Heavy Battalion. Note the complete absence of vision ports in the cupola! Commanders and crew alike would have very little 'situational awareness' buttoned up in a vehicle like this, although the Turan II's reportedly performed very well against Russian T34's and the like. The cover plate for the hole in the glacis can be seen lying in front of the vehicle. **RGAKFD**

The same vehicle as on Page 55 but from the rear. Most of the Turán II's had brackets to hold turret and hull side skirts for added protection. The thin armour on Turáns (13-50 mm) was equivalent to that found on a Pz.Kpfw.IV Ausf.D at the start of WW2. The tactical number '3211' can be seen on the turret rear. Note the cross (white on a black square) on the side of the superstructure.

RGAKFD

Another Turán II with the skirts fitted followed by another Turán I. Spare roadwheels were carried on either side of the rear plate and large access hatches opened up the engine compartment. (In this photo, you can see the armour over the engine compartment has been dislodged and moved over.) The tactical number for this vehicle, '32', can be seen on page 58. It is possible that the nine Turán tanks seen here were damaged when the Hungarian 2nd Armoured Division fought against the Russians in the Vértes Hills west of Budapest.

RGAKFD

This photo reveals the extensive damage done to the vehicle's right hand side where both track and roadwheels have been shot through. A small cross again appears on the side of the superstructure. Further along are two more Turán I's.

RGAKFD

On the left is a Turán II which carried tactical number '2101' on its turret rear and registration number '2H227' painted on the edge of the louvred cover on the top right hand side of the engine deck. Behind it is a rather 'late' Turán II with half of its skirts mounted and half of them missing. It carried tactical number '3112' on the turret rear and an inverted triangle on its front plate and has been shot up and burnt out. The last vehicle in line can be seen in more detail on the next page. **RGAKFD**

A rear shot of a 'late' Turán II, with tactical number '56' on its turret skirts and registration number '242 H2' on the bottom rear plate. Rather than being a solid plate or made of wire mesh, the skirting plate was a thin flat plate perforated with thousands of fine holes. Leaving the hull skirts attached during rail transport would have all but insured their damage or loss. Note the smoke dischargers on the rear plate next to the spare road wheel. **RGAKFD**

A Pz.Kpfw.M15 from Pz.Abt.202 lies overturned in Hungary, March 1945. The official caption with the photograph gives the location as the Nagykanizsa area, but it could also be on the northen bank of the river Drava, as the Abteilung fought at the Drávaszabolcs bridgehead. The drive sprocket has four retainers fixed to the outside, a German modification to keep the track on the sprocket. The stowage bins on the back of the turret and engine deck are particular to vehicles of Pz.Abt.202. More vehicles unique to this unit can be found in *Panzerwrecks 2*.

MPAB

A dead 'Hummel', this one photographed in Brieg (now Brzeg in Poland), after it fell to Russian forces on 6 February 1945. Like the other examples shown in this book, the rear superstructure has disappeared leaving only the gun mount and warped hull plates. The vehicle has the remains of a whitewash over the paintwork. The rear tyres have been burnt to ash. Our best guess for whom it belonged to is the II./Pz.Art.Rgt.16 of 16.Panzer-Division who were in the area of Breslau (now Wroclaw) in late January. **RGAKFD**

What is thought to be the mount of the Abteilung commander of the s.H.Pz.Abt.509, was blown up on 25 March 1945 near Lake Balaton due to broken final drives. The tank is interesting as it is a rare example of a Tiger outfitted as a Panzerbefehlswagen Tiger Ausf.B (Sd.Kfz.268) and would have carried an extra antenna on the turret roof (part of the base is just visible behind the loader's periscope). Spare antennas for the FuG 7 were stowed in a cylindrical stowage bin at the back of the engine deck, above and between the exhaust pipes as seen here. A 'Jerrycan' in a rack has been fitted on the rear plate next to the exhaust pipe.

Positive unit ID for this Tiger II is difficult as both the s.H.Pz.Abt.503 and s.H.Pz.Abt.509 were known to mount a third set of spare tracks on the turret sides. An explosion has popped open the welds between the front and side armour, buckled the plate over the driver's and radio operator's position and burnt out the vehicle so badly that the suspension has sagged to the ground. The tank was destroyed in Hungary, 1945.

This whitewashed Tiger II from an unidentified unit has suffered a fire which has softened the torsion bar suspension, making the tank belly out on the ground. The fire has also caused some of the 'Zimmerit' coating to flake off of the side of the turret. The number '300' is a Russian addition. It appears that the crew had drained the recuperator fluid and fired a final round leaving the gun at full recoil and therefore useless to its captors.

Panzer IV/70(V) tactical number '122' has ended up stuck in the mud. The crew have opened the right engine access hatch revealing the large cooling fans - note how dark the interior of the engine bay is, this would have been painted in Rot RAL 8012. An interesting detail is that the tanker's bar has been used to open the hatch, as it is still there, poking out of the side.

A thoroughly destroyed Panzer IV/70(A) photographed in Hungary. Like the vehicle shown on page 43, this one has four return rollers which are just about visible in the shadows. The side and rear armour have separated at the weld seam because of an internal explosion, this has also blown off the roof and some of the hatches on the engine deck. One 'Flammentöter' exhaust remains on the rear plate.

A naked Tiger II basks in the Spring sunshine around Lake Balaton, Hungary in 1945. It would not have been too far away from the Tiger '300' on page 65 as this one has the number '307a'. We get a good view of the sagging torsion bars as all the roadwheels have disappeared, in fact pretty much everything that could be removed has been removed including the hatches, gun shield and muzzle brake, making us think that perhaps this was not the work of looters, but the 'I-Staffel'.

A Jagdpanzer IV in Bulgarian use, complete with large red, white edged star. The vehicle has been repainted in Russian green. The vehicle is pretty much standard issue although the ice cleats on the tracks are an addition. Note the lack of 'Zimmerit' on the rear plate. This vehicle, like those on pages 70 and 71 was received from the Soviets in late March of 1945. In front is a Hungarian built Turán.

MPAB

A Pz.Kpfw.IV Ausf.H or J in Bulgarian hands. This tank was not one of the 91 delivered from Germany between 1943-44 but supplied by the Russians. Barely discernible in the background of the inset photo is the Jagdpanzer 38 on the next page. **2x MPAB**

A Bulgarian crewed Jagdpanzer 38 at speed. A makeshift track guard has been fitted to the right side of the vehicle and a 'Bosch' headlamp replaces the more usual 'Notek' lamp. A few spare links of track are stowed between the hull and Schürzen. **MPAB**

How do you make a Pz.Kpfw.IV look like an Elefant? By taking away the return rollers. This late version Ausf.J, with 'Drahtgeflecht-Schürzen' (wire mesh skirts) and extended side armour towing points, has been thoroughly destroyed and pushed into a roadside ditch in Hungary. The tank is devoid of national markings and tactical numbers, which is unusual. Along the track guard we can clearly see the two position brackets for the 'Schürzen'.

Another late Pz.Kpfw.IV Ausf.J, again with mesh ‘Schürzen’ and extended side tow points. The turret front lacks the gunner’s direct vision port - a feature of many late Ausf.Js and the front of the armoured recuperator housing is missing the four bolts and now it hangs askew. Comparing the brackets along the track guards with those on page 72, we can see that they are in the position for the ‘Schürzen’ to clear ‘Ostketten’.

The tactical number on the side of this Panzer IV/70(V) starts with a '9' and appears to read '923'. This coupled with the fact that it was knocked out during the Lake Balaton operation leads us to conclude that it belonged to 9./SS-Pz.Rgt.9 of 9.SS-Panzer-Division. The vehicle has ended its days in a puddle, the Russian photographer creatively catching its reflection. It is unusual to see a vehicle of this type with its 'Schürzen' intact.

Another Panzer IV/70(V) from 9./SS-Pz.Rgt.9 (note the barely visible number '9' on the side of the fighting compartment) that has suffered an internal explosion which has blown the roof off the fighting compartment. The vehicle has been 'short-tracked' to avoid the drive sprocket which is presumably damaged. This was standard practice for German recovery units. The sprung gun travel lock should sit flat against the nose armour when not in use; debris must be preventing it from doing so here. Compare the camouflage scheme to the example on page 74.

Tiger '334' is something of a surprise as a few months earlier on 22 December 1944, s.SS-Pz.Abt.501 left Tiger '334' at Borgoumont in Belgium during the Ardennes Offensive where it was photographed by US photographers (see pages 278-279 of *Battle of the Bulge Then and Now*). It shows that at least some losses sustained in the Ardennes were made good before moving to Hungary. *Tigers in Combat 2* states that on 19 March 1945, near Inota, Hungary, several tanks had to be blown up due to a lack of recovery vehicles.

Further down the road lies Tiger '313', again from s.SS-Pz.Abt.501. This tank clearly shows the signs of an internal explosion: sagging suspension from fire, blown out driver's and radio operator's hatch plate and missing commander's hatch. It is notable that the gun is at full recoil as well. Note that the spare track links extend above the top of the turret sides.

A wrecked Tiger sits, minus its exhausts, muzzle brake, left track and part of the turret roof, at Pillau (now Baltiysk) harbour, April 1945. Given the location it is highly likely that this was the mount of Fw. Albert Kerscher of 2./s.H.Pz.Abt.511 who blew up his tank on 24 April 1945 in the harbour area. By this date the s.H.Pz.Abt.511 was down to just 3 tanks.
TsAMO

Russian soldiers pose with a Tiger I hull at the end of 1944 or beginning of 1945. This was most likely a training vehicle since apart from it lacking a turret, it has no radio operator's ball mounted MG. Several roadwheels and other items are also missing. Barely visible in the background are the wrecks of Pz.Kpfw.III and Pz.Kpfw.IV training vehicles. **L.Archer**

A T-26 lies wrecked on the banks of the river Daugava in Latvia. It is relatively uncommon to find images of the T-26 in German use, and more so with a post 1943 camouflage pattern. Although we do not know the unit, it was likely that the little tank belonged to a Police or anti partisan unit. The photograph has been retouched by the Russians, which explains the odd look of the running gear.

LVKFFDA 69447N

Partisans of the 1st Kovpak Ukrainian Partisan Division inspect their handiwork, a knocked out ADGZ armoured car, in January 1944. The vehicle had been whitewashed and had been carrying planks of wood across the front, why?
3x RGAKFD

A RSO/01 turned colander at Mariampol, Lithuania, in the Summer of 1944. Despite the thorough destruction of the RSO, the Pak40 that it had been towing has come off relatively unscathed. There is at least one 7.5cm shell among the surrounding detritus possibly indicating that the RSO had been carrying ammunition. The gun has no camouflage pattern and has wire threaded around the bolts on the gun shield to hold camouflage materials. **RGAKFD**

A Bulgarian soldier peers into the empty void that once housed the V-8 engine of a late version Ford V3000 Maultier. Pretty much everything of use has been removed from the vehicle, even down to the lights, seats and windows. The camouflage pattern has been applied by brush over the RAL 7028 Dunkelgelb basecoat. More examples of Ford V3000 Maultiers can be seen in *Panzerwrecks 3*. **2x MPAB**

Opposite page: German and Romanian prisoners of war are marched past a pair of 'Hummels' and Sturmgeschütz in Sevastopol, Ukraine, 1944. The two 'Hummels' have been camouflaged with red-brown or green sprayed in lines over the RAL 7028 Dunkelgelb basecoat, the two Sturmgeschütz have been left in plain Dunkelgelb. **This page**: A Sturmgeschütz Ausf.F, several Ausf.G's and a Marder II at what is probably the same weapons park.
2x RGAKFD

A Sturmhaubitze 42 and Pz.Kpfw.M15 photographed in Belgrade on 5 January 1945 by a Bulgarian photographer. The Pz.Kpfw.M15, probably from Pz.Abt.z.b.V.12, has extra ventilation courtesy of a slab of armour missing from the turret. Like the M15 in *Panzerwrecks 4*, it has the amoeba camouflage pattern. **2x MPAB**

The howitzer on this StuH 42 has taken a direct hit, shearing off its muzzle brake. It has a coaxial MG opening in the gun mantlet, but lacks the extra protection in front of the commander's cupola. It is most likely that it belonged to 1.Battr.H.Stu.Gesch.Brig.191 which fought in Belgrade in October 1944. **MPAB**

A B IV c schwere Ladungsträger (Sd.Kfz.301) from Pz.Abt.(FKL)302 sits in a devastated street in Warsaw sometime in 1945. The vehicle has been backed on top of another, whose drive sprocket can be seen in the left of the picture. The pole on the top of the engine compartment had a light on top to assist with guidance of the B IV when under radio control.
RGAKFD

A Russian cameraman filmed the images on pages 89 to 96 as German Forces in Kurland (Courland) surrendered to their captors in May, 1945. Here the crew of a Pz.Kpfw.IV manoeuvre their tank into the designated assembly area, perhaps self conscious about the tracks of Russian tanks that cover their vehicle. **LVKFFDA I-152 (N. Karmazinskis)**

Kurland is the westernmost part of Latvia, and juts into the Baltic Sea and Bay of Riga. If you looked at your right hand, Latvia would be the tip of your right thumb. Lithuania would be below the knuckle, and Germany would be the wrist. Russian controlled territory in early 1945 would be the rest of your hand. The German forces in Kurland withstood six separate Russian offensives during the war and, at the time of surrender, approximated 200,000 German troops were still isolated there, Hitler having refused to evacuate them while they could still draw Russians forces away from Berlin. Although they missed the inferno of Berlin, they faced captivity in Russia. Here the decorated tank commander salutes. **LVKFFDA I-152 (N. Karmazinskis)**

An impressive line up of Pz.Kpfw.IV's, some draped with covers as if their crews would soon return. For reasons unknown, tank number '404' has had three bolts welded to the turret roof and it looks like dirt has been shovelled onto the roof of the driver's compartment. Note that the doors on the turret skirt armour have had their inner faces camouflaged to match the outside scheme, and that several track links are sandwiched between the 'Schürzen' and turret side. Adding interest are two pairs of socks draped on the gun barrel. The second and fifth vehicles in line have shallow boxes on their roofs.

LVKFFDA I-152 (N. Karmazinskis)

These vehicles are believed to have belonged to 12.Panzer-Division based on its status report dated 1.3.45, which recorded the following AFVs: II./Pz.Rgt.29 (5. - 8. Kp) had 61 Pz. IV L/48. 1 Pz. IV L/24, 2 Bef.Pz. III, and 3 Pz. III 5cm L/60. Pz.Jg.Abt. 2 (1. + 2. Kp) had 22 Jagdpz IV L/48 and 6 StuG III (no other unit in Kurland had these tank destroyers.) 1./PzArt. Rgt.2 had 2 Pz. IV L/48, 1 Pz. IV L/24, 2 Pz III 5cm L/60, 1 Pz.Bef. III 5cm L/42. 3 Hummel, 1 Mun-Hummel, 10 Wespe, and 2 Mun-Wespe. Note the metal frames built above the fighting compartments of several of the 'Wespe'. The Beute panzers shown here (T34's, SU85 and Sherman) could have belonged to any of several units in Kurland.

4x LVKFFDA I-152 (N. Karmazinskis)

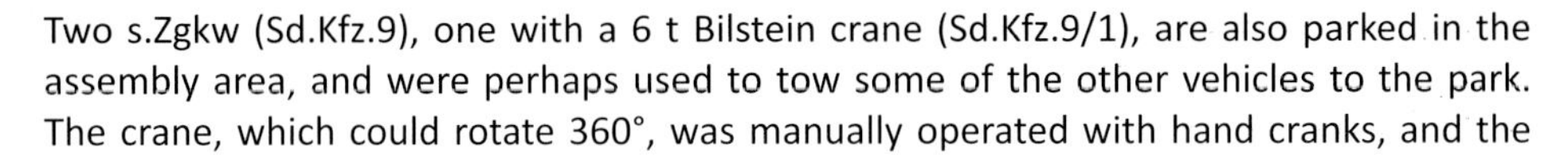

Two s.Zgkw (Sd.Kfz.9), one with a 6 t Bilstein crane (Sd.Kfz.9/1), are also parked in the assembly area, and were perhaps used to tow some of the other vehicles to the park. The crane, which could rotate 360°, was manually operated with hand cranks, and the telescoping boom was held in a crutch when traveling. What look like trays, possibly from the rear toolbox, are piled up behind the crane.

4x LVKFFDA I-152 (N. Karmazinskis)

A line up of recon vehicles. Several of those in the foreground are schwere Panzerspähwagen (Fu) (Sd.Kfz.232) with a 'Sternantenne' for their powerful radios mounted on 'Steckmasten' (extension poles). Although covered by tarps, some of the contours of the other AFVs suggest they are the gun armed schwere Panzerspähwagen (7.5cm) Sd.Kfz.233. Since 12.Panzer-Division did not have any of the latter vehicles, it is thought they belonged instead to Pz.A.A.14 of 14.Panzer-Division. The le.SPW Sd.Kfz.250/9's in the background were present in both Pz. A.A.12 and Pz.A.A.14.

LVKFFDA I-152 (N. Karmazinskis)

In the foreground are m.SPW's endemic to most Panzer Divisions. Note the unit insignia on the rear door of one of them. The m.SPW on the far left appears to be a field-modified mittlerer Funkpanzerwagen (Sd.Kfz.251/3) with a slightly crooked 'Sternantenne' / 'Steckmasten' combination. The Jagdpanzer 38's in the background, however, can belong only to H.Pz.Jg.Abt.731. Notice the different muffler configurations on these vehicles. **LVKFFDA I-152 (N. Karmazinskis)**

More Jagdpanzer 38's and more m.SPW's. The second m.SPW in from the left is a mittlerer Funkpanzerwagen (Sd.Kfz.251/3) with its 'Antennenfuß' internally mounted on the right rear corner of the crew compartment. Of more interest is the mittlerer Krankenpanzerwagen (Sd.Kfz.251/8) ambulance in the middle which seems to have a hard roof cover with a small window in the rear, and a mittlerer Schützenpanzerwagen (7.5cm) (Sd.Kfz.251/9) 'Stummel' (fifth vehicle in from the left). At the far end of the top row are three Jagdpanzer IV L/48 tank destroyers.

LVKFFDA I-152 (N. Karmazinskis)